Famous & Fun Pop

12 Appealing Piano Arrangements

Carol Matz

Famous & Fun Pop, Book 2, contains 12 carefully selected popular hits from movies, radio and television. Each piece has been arranged especially for early elementary to elementary pianists, yet remains faithful to the sound of the original. The arrangements can be used as a supplement to any method. No eighth notes or dotted-quarter rhythms are used. The optional duet parts for teacher or parent add to the fun. Enjoy your experience with these popular hits!

Carol Matz

The Chicken Dance

(a.k.a. Dance Little Bird)

Words and Music by
Terry Rendall and Werner Thomas
Arranged by Carol Matz

DUET PART (Student plays one octave higher)

(Meet) The F

A Whole New World

(from Walt Disney's "Aladdin")

Words by Tim Rice
Music by Alan Menken
Arranged by Carol Matz

Flowing quickly

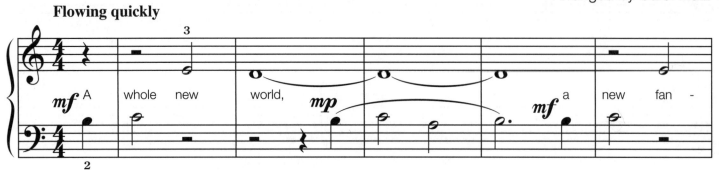

whole new world, a new fan -

DUET PART (Student plays one octave higher)

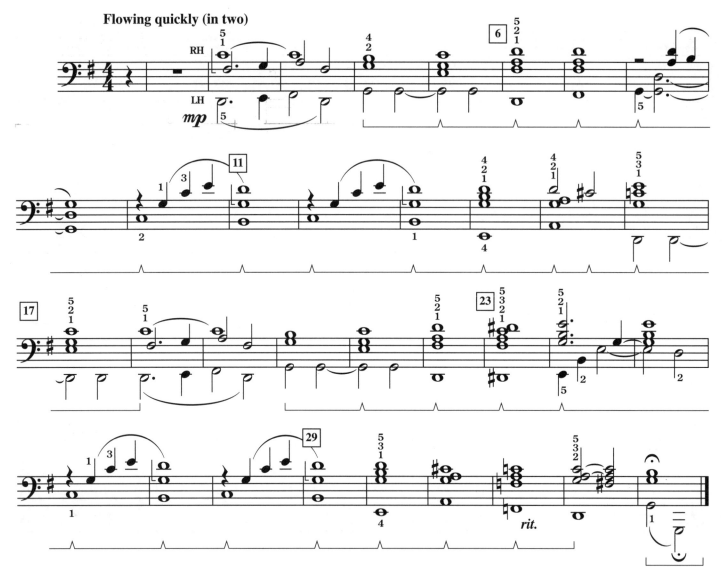

6

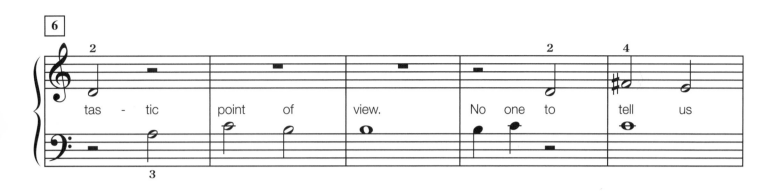

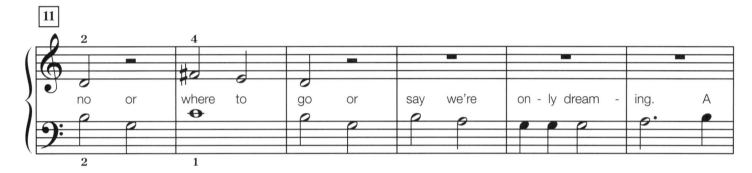

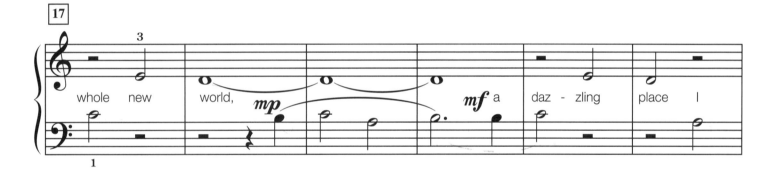

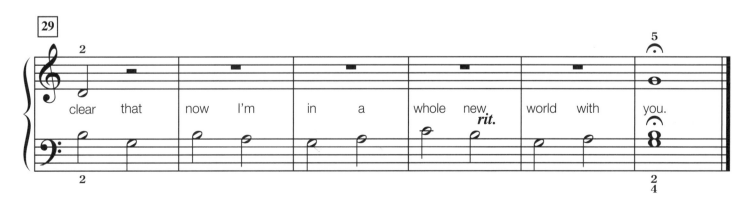

8

Star Wars
(Main Title)

Music by **JOHN WILLIAMS**
Arranged by Carol Matz

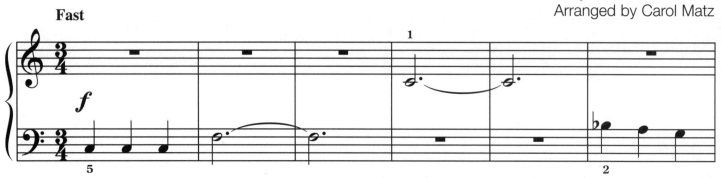

DUET PART (Student plays one octave higher)

It's My Party

Words and Music by
Herb Wiener, Seymour Gottlieb,
John Gluck, Jr. and Wally Gold
Arranged by Carol Matz

Moderately

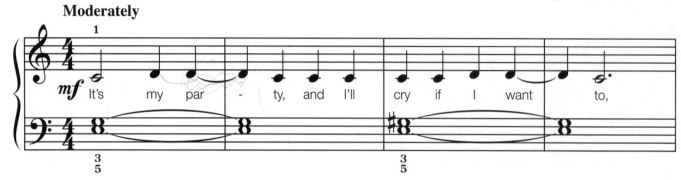

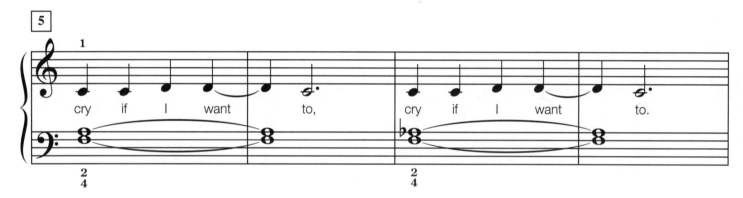

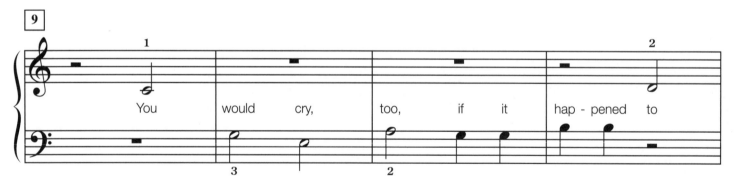

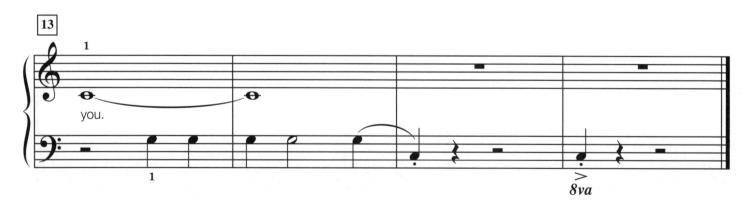

Great Balls of Fire

Words and Music by
Otis Blackwell and Jack Hammer
Arranged by Carol Matz

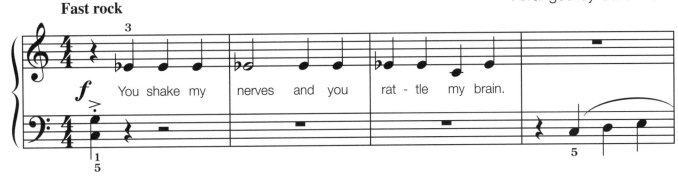

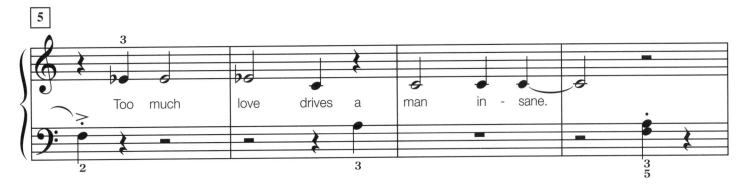

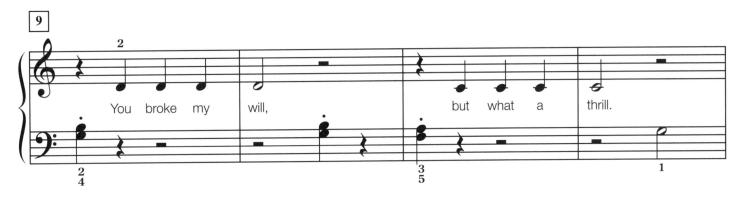

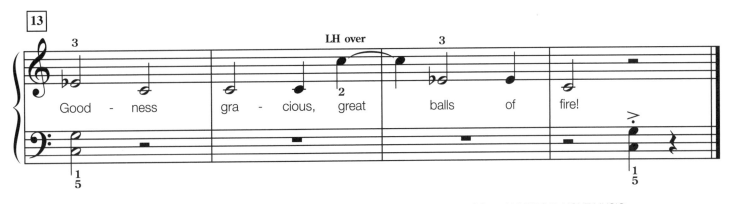

Merrily We Roll Along

Words and Music by
Eddie Cantor, Charlie Tobias and Murray Mencher
Arranged by Carol Matz

DUET PART (Student plays one octave higher)

Zip-a-Dee-Doo-Dah

(from Walt Disney's "Song of the South")

Words by Ray Gilbert
Music by Allie Wrubel
Arranged by Carol Matz

*Great, Veral.
Review for Hol
Feb. 2*

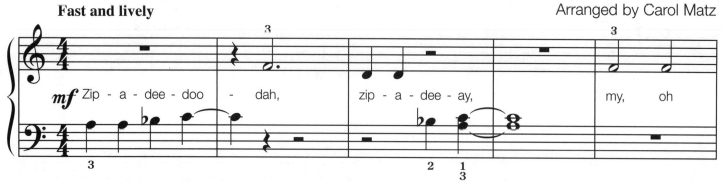

DUET PART (Student plays one octave higher)

Talk to the Animals

Words and Music by Leslie Bricusse
Arranged by Carol Matz

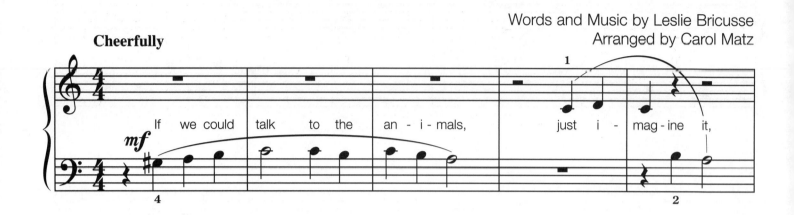

DUET PART (Student plays one octave higher)

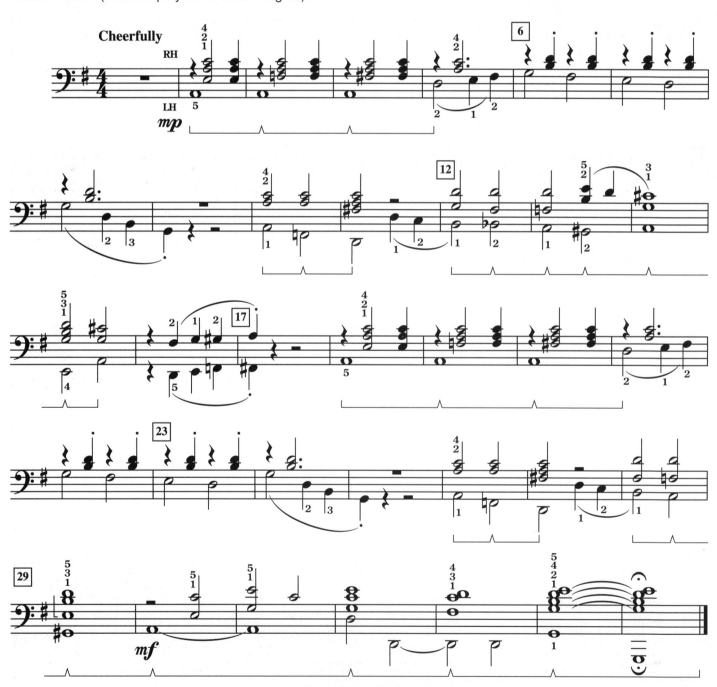

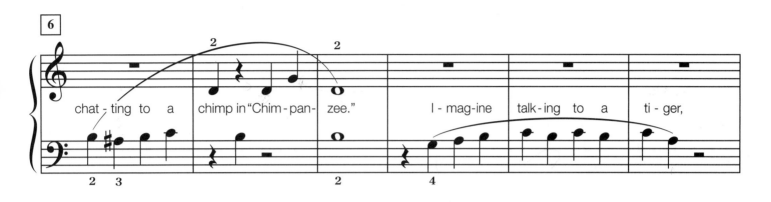

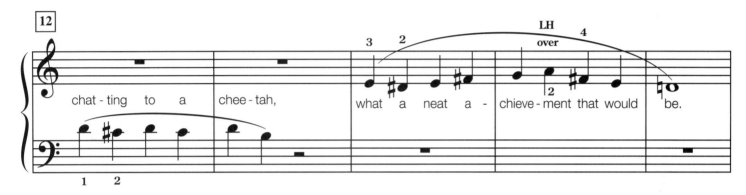

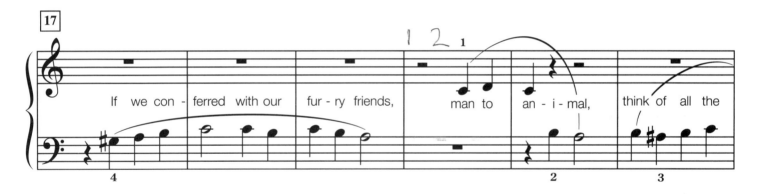

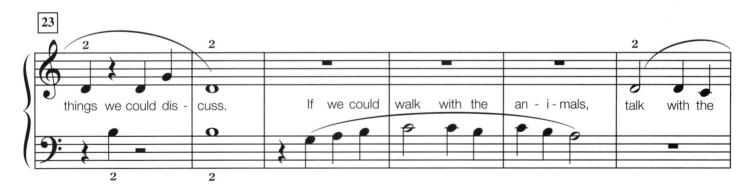

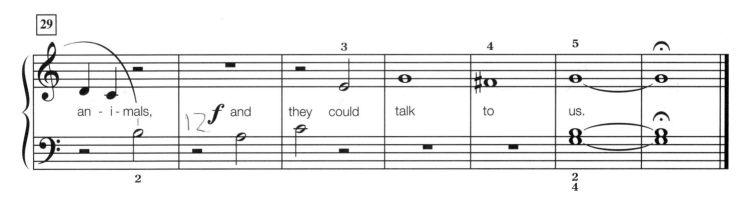

If I Only Had a Brain

(featured in the M-G-M Picture "The Wizard of Oz")

Music by Harold Arlen
Lyric by E. Y. Harburg
Arranged by Carol Matz

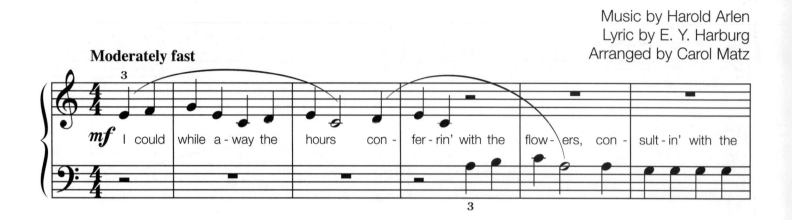

DUET PART (Student plays one octave higher)

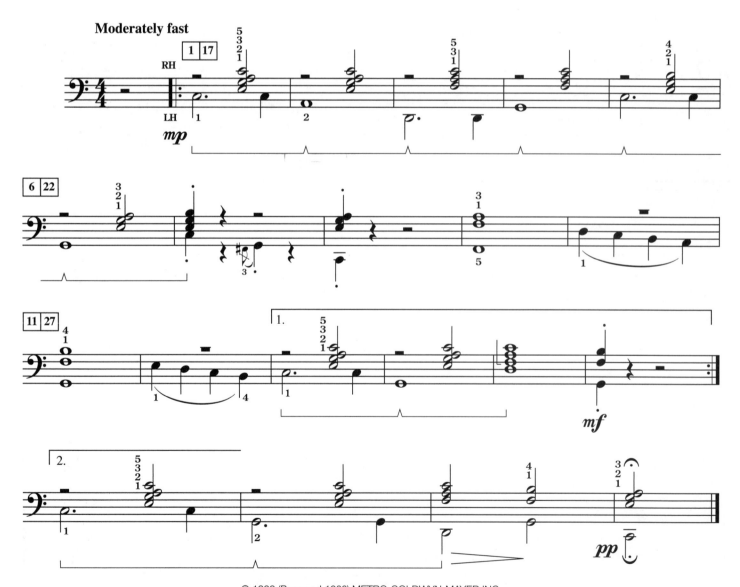

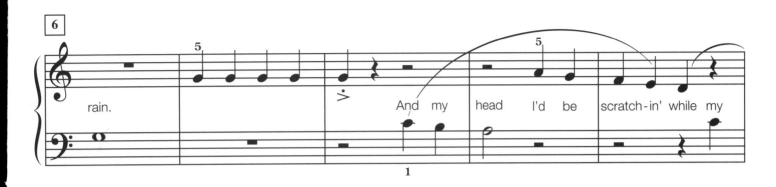

rain.   And my   head   I'd be   scratch-in' while my

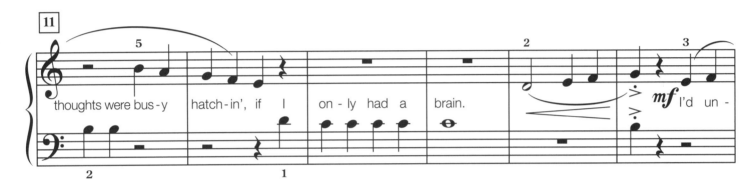

thoughts were bus-y   hatch-in', if I   on - ly had a   brain.   *mf* I'd un -

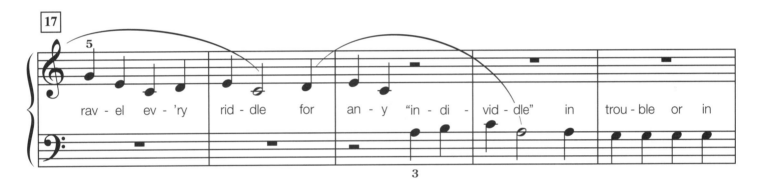

rav - el ev - 'ry   rid - dle   for   an - y "in - di - vid - dle"   in   trou - ble or in

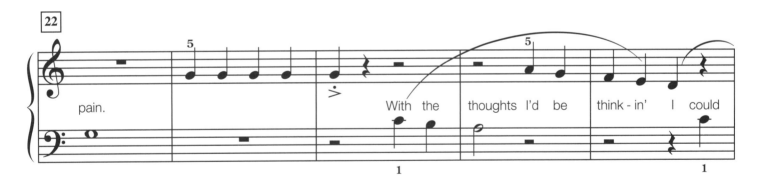

pain.   With the   thoughts I'd be   think - in' I could

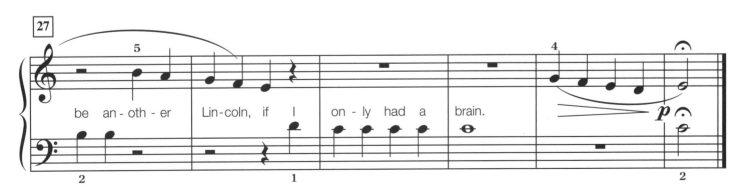

be an - oth - er   Lin - coln, if I   on - ly had a   brain.   *p*

The James Bond Theme

Music by Monty Norman
Arranged by Carol Matz

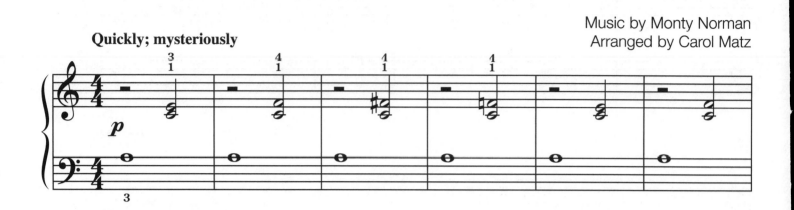

DUET PART (Student plays one octave higher)

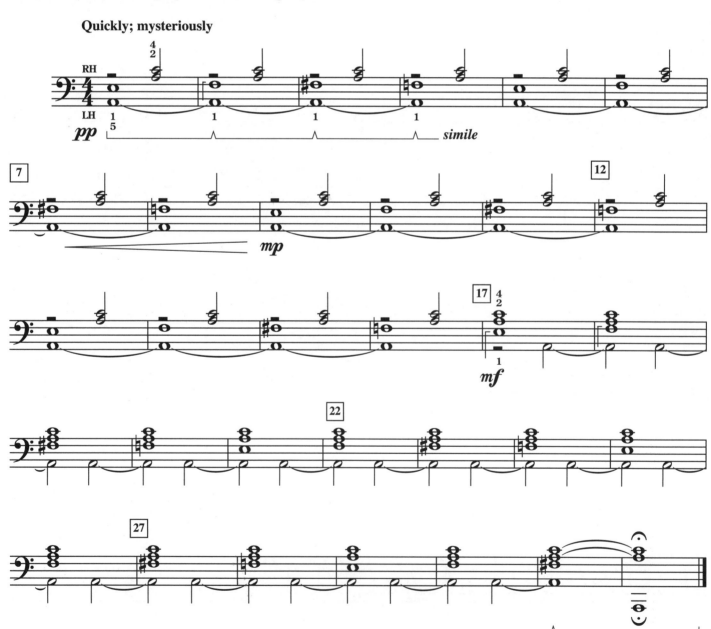

Featured in the M-G-M Picture "The Wizard of Oz"

We're Off to See the Wizard

(The Wonderful Wizard of Oz)

Music by Harold Arlen
Lyric by E. Y. Harburg
Arranged by Carol Matz

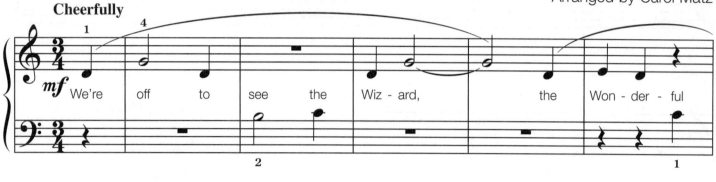

We're off to see the Wiz - ard, the Won - der - ful

DUET PART (Student plays one octave higher)

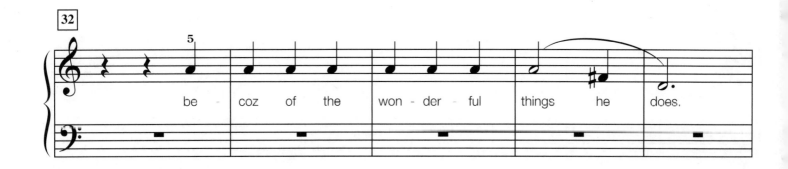

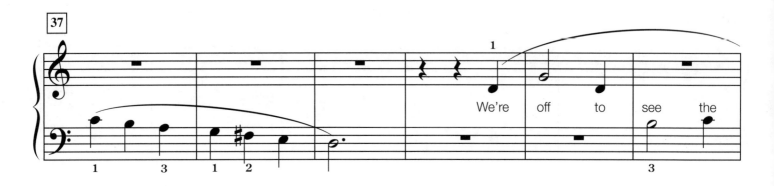

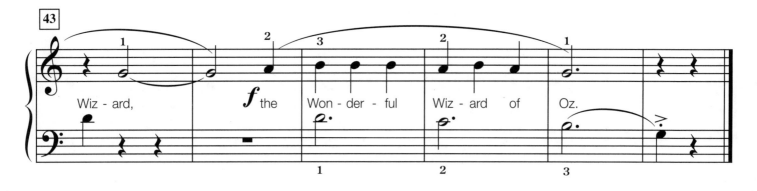

DUET PART (continued)

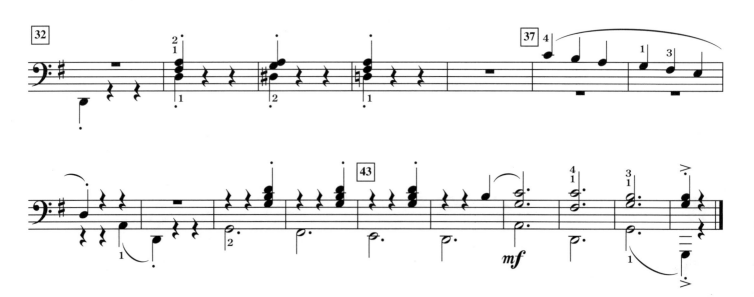